2

LET'S GO

Student Book

by
R. Nakata
K. Frazier

with
songs by Carolyn Graham

Oxford University Press

Oxford University Press

198 Madison Avenue
New York, NY 10016 USA

Great Clarendon Street
Oxford OX2 6DP England

Oxford New York
Athens Auckland Bangkok Bogota Bombay Buenos Aires
Calcutta Cape Town Dar es Salaam Delhi Florence Hong Kong
Istanbul Karachi Kuala Lumpur Madras Madrid Melbourne
Mexico City Nairobi Paris Singapore Taipei Tokyo Toronto Warsaw

and associated companies in
Berlin Ibadan

OXFORD is a trademark of Oxford University Press.

ISBN 0-19-434397-9

Senior Editor: Shelagh Speers
Associate Editor: John Hurlin
Senior Designer: April Okano
Art Buyer/Picture Researcher: Karen Polyak
Production Manager: Abram Hall

Cover design by April Okano
Cover illustrations by Paul Meisel and Patrick Merrell

Continuing characters illustrated by Dora Leder. Other
interior illustrations by Shirley Beckes, Patrick Girouard, Maj-
Britt Hagsted, Anne Kennedy, Paul Meisel, Susan Miller, Roz
Schanzer, Maggie Swanson, and Stan Tusan.

Printing (last digit): 20 19 18 17 16 15 14

Printed in Hong Kong.

Icons

Every unit in Let's Go 2 is divided into six lessons, with additional review after every two units. Each lesson is identified by a colorful icon. The same icons are used for reference on corresponding pages in the Teacher's Book and Workbook.

Let's Talk
Functional dialogue

Let's Read
Reading skills development

Let's Sing
Interactive song based on the dialogue

Let's Listen
Listening test and unit review

Let's Learn
New grammatical structure

Let's Review
Further review after every two units

Let's Learn Some More
Related grammatical structure

Table of Contents

Let's Talk

Hi, Scott. How are you?

Fine, thank you.

Good-bye, Scott.

See you later.

Good-bye.
See you later.

 **Let's Sing**

Scott

Lisa

♪ **The Hi Song**

Hi, Scott. How are you?
　　I'm fine. Thank you.
Hi, Jenny. How are you?
　　I'm fine. Thank you.
Hi, John. How are you?
　　I'm fine. Thank you.
Hi, Lisa. How are you?
　　I'm fine.

Jenny

John

♪ **The Good-bye Song**

Good-bye, Scott.
　　See you later, alligator!
Good-bye, Kate.
　　See you later, alligator!
Good-bye, Andy.
　　See you later, alligator!
See you later.
　　See you later.
Good-bye, Scott!

Andy

Kate

 # Let's Learn

Ask and answer.

What is	this?	It is a desk.
	that?	

What is = What's
It is = It's

a pencil case
a book
a bag
a desk
a door
a window
a table
a chair

Yes or no?

Is | this | a crayon?   Yes, it is.   is not = isn't
   | that | No, it is not.

a ruler

a book

a notebook

a cassette

a pen

a crayon

an eraser

a marker

Let's Learn Some More

Ask and answer.

What are | these?   They are puzzles.
         | those?

They are = They're

balls

puzzles

cars

yo-yos

bicycles

bats

kites

jump ropes

10

Yes or no?

| Are | these | frogs? | Yes, they are. |
| | those | | No, they are not. |

are not = aren't

cats

dogs

spiders

flowers

trees

birds

frogs

rabbits

Let's Read

Word Families

- at	- an	- ap
cat	can	cap
fat	fan	lap
hat	van	map

Can you read?

The fat cat is in the hat.

The can and the fan are on the van.

The cap and the map are on my lap.

Let's Listen

1.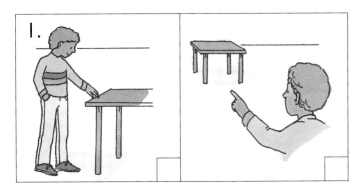

2.

3.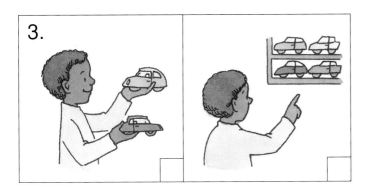

4.

5.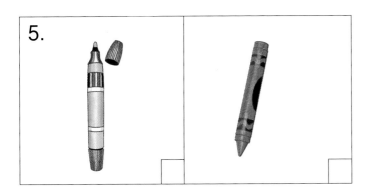

6.

7.

8.

Let's Talk

What is the matter?
I am sick.
That is too bad.

What is = What's
I am = I'm
That is = That's

What's the Matter?

What's the matter?
What's the matter?
What's the matter?
    I am sick.
What's the matter? Are you OK?
    I am sick today.
Oh, no!
What's the matter?
    I am very, very sick today.
Oh, no!
    I am very, very, very, very sick today.
That's too bad!

sad

hot

tired

cold

Let's Learn

Ask and answer.

| Who is | he ? | He | is | Mr. Hill. | He | is a cook. |
| | she? | She | | | She | |

Who is = Who's
He is = He's
She is = She's

Mr. Hill
a cook

Mr. White
a taxi driver

Miss Smith
a nurse

Mr. Jones
a farmer

Miss Bates
a shopkeeper

Mr. Bell
a police officer

Rita
a student

Mrs. Lee
a teacher

Yes or no?

Is | he / she | a teacher?   Yes, | he / she | is.   No, | he / she | is not.   is not = isn't

   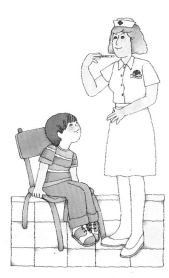

What about you?

I am a _____ .

Let's Learn Some More

Ask and answer.

Who are they?   They are Mr. and Mrs. Long.
They are teachers.

They are = They're

cooks   students   farmers

Yes or no?

Are they cooks?   Yes, they are.
                    No, they are not.   are not = aren't

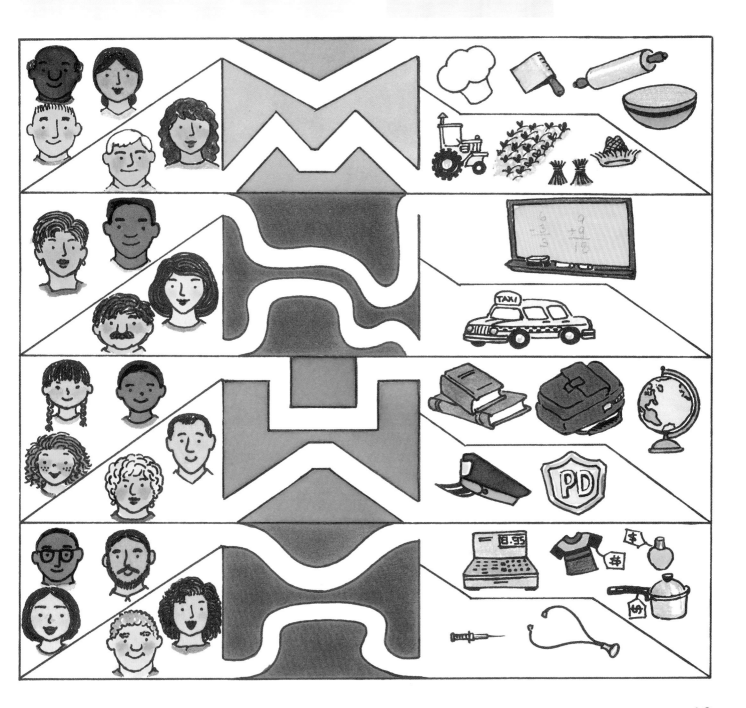

Let's Read

Word Families

-ed	-en	-et
bed	hen	net
red	pen	pet
Ted	ten	wet

Can you read?

Ted is in the red bed.

The ten pens are by the hen.

The wet pet is in the net.

Let's Listen

1.

2.

3.

4.

5.

6.

7.

8.

Let's Review

1. Say these.

2. Listen carefully.

a.

b.

3. Say and act.

4. Answer the question.

Are those dogs?

☐ Yes, they are.
☐ No, they are not.

Are they nurses?

☐ Yes, they are.
☐ No, they are not.

Is he a police officer?

☐ Yes, he is.
☐ No, he is not.

5. Listen and read. Circle the word.

a.  This
That is a notebook.

c.   He
She is a cook.

b.  These
Those are cats.

d.  These
They are pens.

Let's Talk

Where do you live?
I live in Hillsdale.

Let's Sing

123-4456

♪ The Telephone Number Song

What's your telephone number?
What's your telephone number?
What's your telephone number?
    123-4456
    That's my telephone number.

What's his telephone number?
What's his telephone number?
What's his telephone number?
    655-4321
    That's his telephone number.

What's her telephone number?
What's her telephone number?
What's her telephone number?
    242-4668
    That's her telephone number.

655-4321

242-4668

Let's Learn

This is my house.
This is the bedroom.

bedroom

kitchen

dining room

living room

bathroom

26

Ask and answer.

Where is the bed?   It is in the bedroom.

Where is = Where's
It is = It's

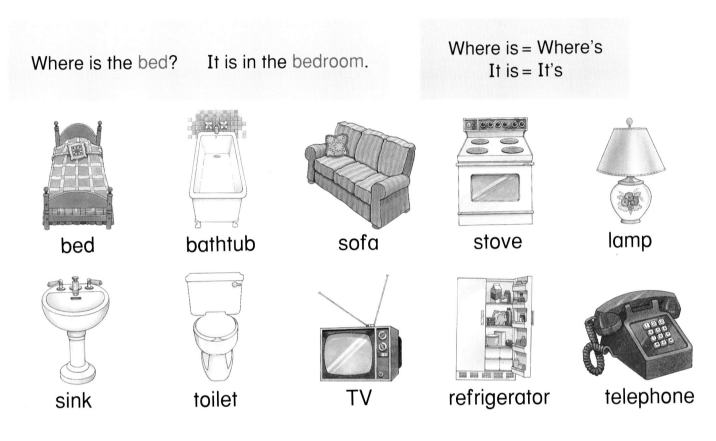

bed   bathtub   sofa   stove   lamp

sink   toilet   TV   refrigerator   telephone

Yes or no?

Is the desk in the bedroom?   Yes, it is.
No, it is not.

is not = isn't

Let's Learn Some More

next to   in front of   behind

There is a lamp next to the sofa.   There are lamps behind the sofa.

Practice.

There is a chair next to the table.   There is = There's

Practice.

There are books under the bed .

in
on
under
in front of
behind
next to

Yes or no?

Are there books on the chair?   Yes, there are.
No, there are not.

Is there a TV on the table?   Yes, there is.
No, there is not.

is not = isn't
are not = aren't

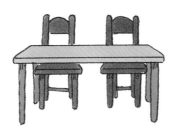

 # Let's Read

Word Families

-in	-it	-ig
fin	hit	big
pin	pit	fig
thin	sit	twig

Can you read?

The pin is in the thin fin.	Hit the ball and sit in the pit.	The fig is on the big twig.

Let's Listen

1.

2.

3.

4.

5.

6.

7.

8.

Let's Talk

What is wrong?
    I cannot find my book.

What is = What's
cannot = can't

Let's Sing

♪ What's Wrong?

What's wrong, Andy?
    I can't find my book.
What's wrong, Andy?
    I can't find my book.

    I can't hear the teacher.
    I can't reach the bookshelf.
    I can't find my pencil.
    I can't see the board.
Oh, Andy!

He can't hear the teacher.
He can't reach the bookshelf.
He can't find his pencil.
He can't see the board.

Let's Learn

Look at me!
I can do a magic trick.

Look at her!
She can ride a pony.

Practice.

| Look at | me.
him.
her. | I
He
She | can sing a song. |

sing a song

ride a pony

speak English

use chopsticks

write the alphabet

do a magic trick

34

Ask and answer.

| What can | he | do? | He | can | ride a bicycle. |
| | she | | She | | |

What about you?

I can _____ .
I can't _____ .

Let's Learn Some More

She can sing a song, but she cannot dance.

Practice

| He | can swim, but | he | cannot fly a kite. |
| She | | she | |

cannot = can't

Yes or no?

Can | he / she | swim?   Yes, | he / she | can.   No, | he / she | cannot.

cannot = can't

  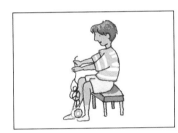 

Ask your friend.

Can you _____ ?

Yes				
No				

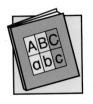 # Let's Read

Word Families

-og	-op	-un
dog	mop	fun
frog	stop	run
log	top	sun

Can you read?

The dog and the frog are on the log.

Stop the top. It is by the mop.

It is fun in the sun. I can run.

Let's Listen

Let's Review

1. Say these.

10 POINTS

2. Listen carefully.

a.

b.

3. Ask your partner.

What can you do?

I can _____ , but I can't _____ .

40

4. Say and act.

Where do you live?

?

I can't find my book.

5. Answer the question.

Can he do a magic trick?

☐ Yes, he can.
☐ No, he cannot.

Can she write the alphabet?

☐ Yes, she can.
☐ No, she cannot.

6. Listen and read. Circle the word.

a.  There is a table next to / in front of the bed.

b. There are lamps next to / behind the sofa.

Let's Talk

Do you want spaghetti?
    Yes, please.
    No, thank you.

♪ Let's Sing

♪ The Spaghetti Song

Do you like spaghetti?
   Yes, I do.
I do, too.
   I do, too.
Do you like spaghetti?
   Yes, I do.
I like spaghetti, too.

Do you want spaghetti?
   Yes, I do.
I do, too.
   I do, too.
Do you want spaghetti?
   Yes, I do.
I want spaghetti, too.

Let's Learn

Practice

What does	he	want?	He	wants an egg.
	she		She	

Yes or no?

Does	he she	want	a salad?	Yes,	he she	does.

No, | he
she | does not.

does not = doesn't

What about you?

I want _____ .

Let's Learn Some More

Ask and answer.

What does | he | like?   He | likes hamburgers.
          | she | She |

hamburgers

oranges

salads

eggs

sandwiches

bananas

hot dogs

cookies

Yes or no?

Does	he	like cookies?	Yes,	he	does.
	she			she	
			No,	he	does not.
				she	

does not = doesn't

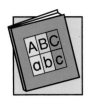

Let's Read

Word Families

-ame	-ake	-ay
game	cake	crayon
name	make	gray
same	snake	play

Can you read?

Can you name the game?

Can a snake make a cake?

Play with a crayon.

Let's Listen

Let's Talk

Whose watch is it?
It is Andy's watch.

It is = It's

Let's Sing

♪ Whose Watch Is That?

Whose watch is that?
    It's Jenny's watch.
Whose hat is that?
    It's Jenny's hat.
Whose books are those?
    They're Jenny's books.
Whose cat is that?
    It's Jenny's cat.

It's Andy's watch.
    It's Jenny's watch.
It's Andy's hat.
    It's Jenny's hat.
They're Andy's books.
    They're Jenny's books.
It's Andy's cat.
    It's Jenny's cat.

Let's Learn

What do you have in your bag?

I have a notebook.

What do you have?

I have a comic book.

Ask and answer.

What do you have in your bag?   I have a comb.

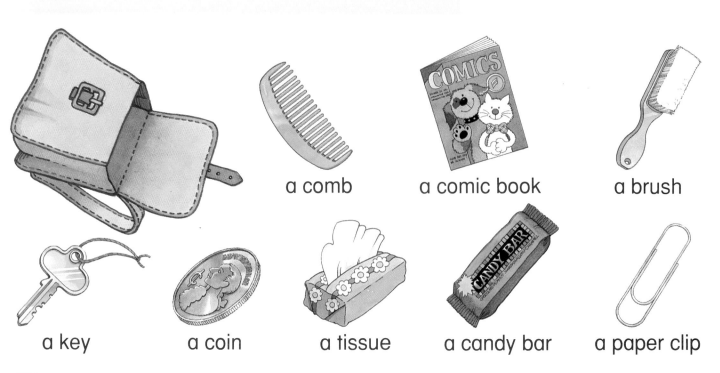

a comb

a comic book

a brush

a key

a coin

a tissue

a candy bar

a paper clip

Yes or no?

Do you have a key in your bag?   Yes, I do.
No, I do not.

do not = don't

What about you?

I have _____ in my bag.

Let's Learn Some More

Ask and answer.

What does	he	have in	his	hand?	He	has a yo-yo
	she		her		She	

54

Yes or no?

Does	he	have a pen in	his	bag?		Yes,	he	does.
	she		her				she	

No, | he | does not.
| she |

does not = doesn't

Let's Read

Word Families

-ea-	-ee-	-e
eat	green	he
ice cream	sleep	she
read	tree	me

Can you read?

Can you read and eat ice cream?

Sleep under the tree.

She likes me.

Let's Listen

1.

2.

3.

4.

5.

6.

7.

8.

Let's Review

1. Say these.

2. Answer the question.

What do you have in your bag?

3. Ask your partner.

Do you want a _____ ?				
Yes				
No				

4. Say and act.

5. Listen carefully.

a.
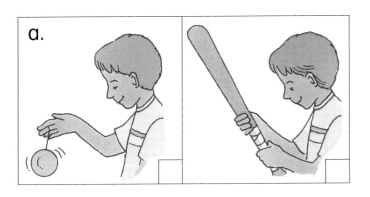

b.

6. Listen and read. Circle the word.

a.  He wants an orange.
egg.

b.  She has a comb.
key.

59

Let's Talk

What time is it?
    It is six o'clock.
    It is time for dinner.

It is = It's

Let's Sing

♪ What Time Is It?

What time is it?
 It's eight o'clock.
 It's time for school. Let's go!
Come on, let's go!
It's time for school.
 It's eight o'clock. Let's go!

What time is it?
 It's twelve o'clock.
 It's time for lunch. Let's go!
Come on, let's go!
It's time for lunch.
 It's twelve o'clock. Let's go!

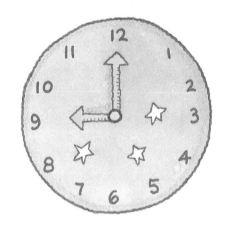

What time is it?
 It's nine o'clock.
 It's time for bed. Let's go!
Come on, let's go!
It's time for bed.
 It's nine o'clock. Let's go!

Let's Learn

Ask and answer.

What do you do in the morning?   I get up.

get up   wash my face   get dressed

brush my teeth   comb my hair   eat breakfast

62

Yes or no?

Do you watch TV in the morning?   Yes, I do.
No, I do not.

do not = don't

morning

afternoon

What about you?

I _____ in the morning.
I _____ in the afternoon.

Let's Learn Some More

Ask and answer.

| What does | he | do in the evening? | He | eats dinner. |
| | she | | She | |

eats

talks

plays

takes

watches

studies

eat dinner

talk on the telephone

play the piano

take a bath

watch TV

study English

Yes or no?

Does | he / she | watch TV at night?

Yes, | he / she | does.

No, | he / she | does not.

does not = doesn't

evening

night

What about you?

I _____ in the evening.

I _____ at night.

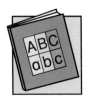

Let's Read

Word Families

-ine	-ice	-ite
line	ice	kite
nine	mice	white
pine	rice	write

Can you read?

Look at the nine pine trees in a line.

Do mice like ice and rice?

Write on the white kite.

Let's Listen

1.

2.

3.

4.

5.

6.

7.

8.

Let's Talk

What are you doing?
   I am combing my hair.

I am = I'm

Let's Sing

♪ What Are You Doing?

What are you doing?
  I'm playing a game.
  Watch what I do,
  And then do the same.

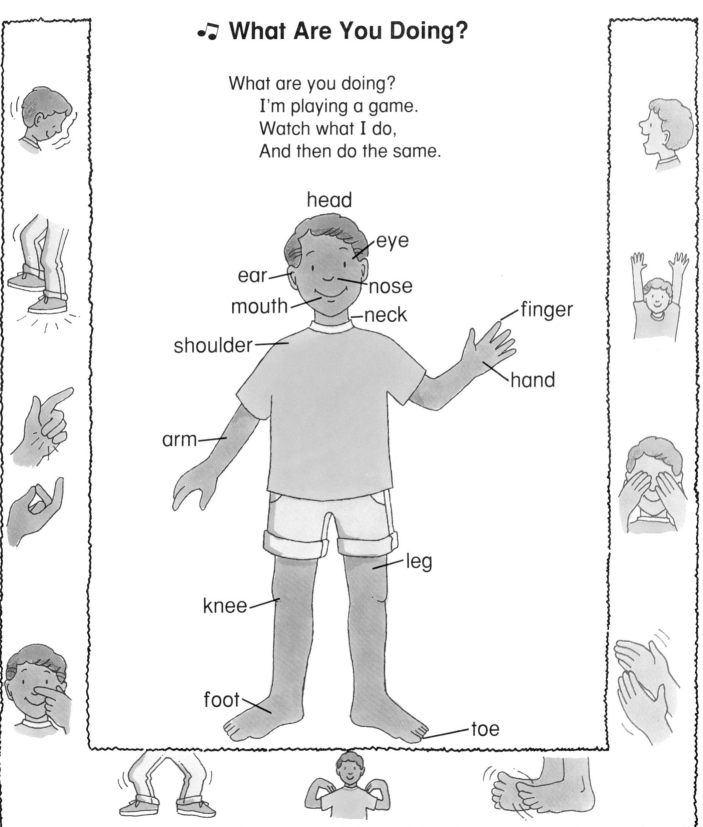

head

eye

ear

nose

mouth

neck

finger

shoulder

hand

arm

leg

knee

foot

toe

Let's Learn

Ask and answer.

What is	he	doing?	He	is swimming.
	she		She	

What is = What's
He is = He's
She is = She's

swimming   sleeping   running

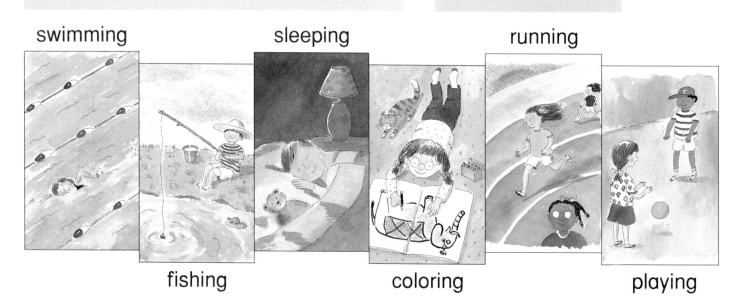

fishing   coloring   playing

Yes or no?

| Is | he
she | coloring? | Yes, | he
she | is. | No, | he
she | is not. |

is not = isn't

What about you?

I am _____ .

Let's Learn Some More

Ask and answer.

Where is | he?   He | is at home.
         | she?   She |

What is | he | doing?   He | is watching TV.
        | she | She |

Where is = Where's
What is = What's
He is = He's
She is = She's

at home

at school

at the store

at the park

Yes or no?

Is | he / she | coloring?　Yes, | he / she | is.　No, | he / she | is not.　　is not = isn't

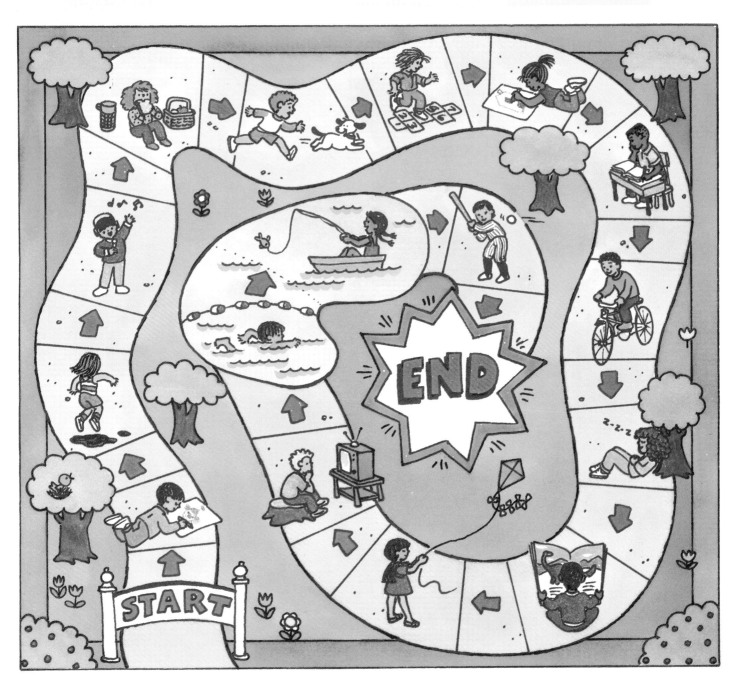

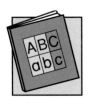 # Let's Read

Word Families

-one	-o	-ue
bone	go	blue
phone	no	Sue
stone	yo-yo	glue

Can you read?

The stone is under the bone by the phone.

No! Go and play with a yo-yo.

Sue's glue is blue.

Let's Listen

1.

2.

3.

4.

5.

6.

7.

8.

Let's Review

1. Say these.

2. Answer the question.

What do you do in the morning?

3. Ask your partner.

Do you _____ in the evening?				
Yes				
No				

4. Say and act.

5. Listen carefully.

6. Listen and read. Circle the word.

a.  She does homework in the evening. / afternoon.

b.  He eats breakfast / dinner in the morning.

Let's Go 2 Syllabus

UNIT	LANGUAGE ITEMS	FUNCTIONS	TOPICS
1	Hi, (Scott). How are you? Fine, thank you. Good-bye, (Scott). See you later. What's this / that? It's (a bag). Is this / that (a pen)? Yes, it is. No, it isn't. What are these / those? They're (jump ropes). Are these / those (dogs)? Yes, they are. No, they aren't.	Greetings Farewells Asking about objects (singular and plural) Identifying objects (singular and plural)	Classroom objects Toys Animals
2	What's the matter? I'm (sick). That's too bad. Who's (she)? (She's) (Miss Day). (She's) (a shopkeeper). Is (she) (a farmer)? Yes, (she) is. No, (she) isn't. Who are they? They're (Mr. and Mrs. Long). They're (teachers). Are they (cooks)? Yes, they are. No, they aren't.	Asking about someone's health Expressing physical states Expressing concern Asking someone else's name Asking about professions Describing professions	Physical states Professions
3	Where do you live? I live in (Hillsdale). What's your address? It's (16 North Street). What's (your) telephone number? It's (798-2043). This is the (living room). Where's the (TV)? It's in the (living room). Is the (stove) in the (bathroom)? Yes, it is. No, it isn't. There is… / There are… Is there…? / Are there…? Yes, there is. No, there isn't. Yes, there are. No, there aren't.	Asking where someone lives Expressing where one lives Asking someone's address / telephone number Expressing one's address / telephone number Identifying rooms in a house Asking about the location of household objects Describing the location of household objects	Addresses Telephone numbers Household objects Rooms in a house
4	What's wrong? I can't (find my book). Look at (me)! (I) can (do a magic trick). What can (she) do? (She) can (speak English). (He) can (sing) but (he) can't (dance). Can (she) (sing a song)? Yes, (she) can. No, (she) can't.	Asking about a problem Expressing ability / inability Describing ability / inability in others	Activities Abilities

UNIT	LANGUAGE ITEMS	FUNCTIONS	TOPICS
5	What's for lunch? (Spaghetti). Do you want (spaghetti)? Yes, please. No, thank you. What about (Scott)? What does (he) want / like? (He) wants (an egg). (He) likes (hamburgers). Does (he) want (a salad)? Does (he) like (cookies)? Yes, (he) does. No, (he) doesn't.	Asking about wants / likes Expressing wants / likes Describing wants / likes of others	Food items
6	Whose (watch) is (that)? It's (Andy's) (watch). Whose (books) are (those)? They're (Jenny's) (books). What do you have in your (bag)? I have (a notebook). Do you have (a pen) in your (bag)? Yes, I do. No, I don't. What does (he) have in (his) (hand)? He has (a frog). Does (she) have (a pen) in (her) (bag)? Yes, (she) does. No, (she) doesn't.	Asking about possession Expressing possession	Personal, everyday objects
7	What time is it? It's (six o'clock). It's time for (dinner). What do you do (in the morning)? I (wash my face) and (comb my hair). Do you (get up) (in the morning)? Yes, I do. No, I don't. What does (she) do (in the evening)? (She) (talks on the telephone). Does (he) (watch TV) (at night)? Yes, (he) does. No, (he) doesn't.	Asking the time Stating the time Asking about daily routine Describing daily routine	Time Times of day Daily activities
8	(Comb your hair). What are you doing? I'm (combing my hair). What's (she) doing? (She's) (playing). Is (she) (swimming)? Yes, (she) is. No, (she) isn't. Where's (he)? (He's) (at the park). Is (he) (coloring)? Yes, (he) is. No, (he) isn't.	Commands Describing what you are doing. Asking what someone else is doing Describing what someone else is doing Asking where someone is Describing where someone is	Parts of the body Activities Locations

Word List

A

a 8
about 17
address 24
afternoon 63
alligator 7
alphabet 34
am 14
an 44
and 12
apple 54
are 6
aren't 11
arm 69
at 34

B

bad 14
bag 8
balls 10
banana 44
bath 60
bathroom 26
bathtub 27
bats 10
bed 20
bedroom 26
behind 28
better 14
bicycles 10
big 30
birds 11
blue 50
board 33
bone 74
book 8
bookshelf 33
breakfast 62
brush 52
brushing 68
but 36
by 20

C

cake 48
can 12,34
candy bar 52
cannot 32
can't 32
cap 12
card 24
cars 10
cassette 9
cat 12
chair 8
chopsticks 34
coin 52
cold 15
coloring 70
comb 52,62
combing 68
come on 61
comic book 52
cook 16

cookie 44
crayon 9

D

dance 36
desk 8
dining room 26
dinner 60
do 24
does 44
doesn't 45
dog 38
doing 68
don't 32
door 8
dressed 62

E

ear 69
eat 56
eats 64
egg 44
eight 60
English 34
eraser 9
evening 64
eye 69

F

face 62
fan 12
farmer 16
fat 12
father 46
fig 30
fin 30
find 32
fine 6
finger 69
fishing 70
flowers 11
fly 36
flying 72
foot 69
for 42
frog 38
front 28
fun 38

G

game 48
get 14
get dressed 62
get up 62
glue 74
go 61
good 42
good-bye 6
good night 60
gray 48
green 50

H

hair 62
hamburger 44
hand 54
has 54
hat 12
have 52
he 16
head 69
hear 33
hello 72
hen 20
her 25
here 32
here's 24
he's 16
hi 6
him 34
his 25
hit 30
home 72
homework 77
hot 15
hot dog 44
house 26
how 6

I

I 14
ice 66
ice cream 56
I'm 7
in 12
in front of 28
is 8
isn't 9
it 8
it's 8

J

jump ropes 10

K

key 52
kitchen 26
kite 66
knee 69
know 32

L

lamp 7
lap 12
later 6
leg 69
let's 61
like 42
likes 46
line 66
live 24
living room 26
log 38
look 34
lunch 42

M

magic trick 34
make 48
map 12
marker 9
matter 14
me 34
mice 66
Miss 16
Mom 32
mop 38
morning 62
mouth 69
Mr. 16
Mrs. 16
my 25

N

name 48
neck 69
net 20
next to 28
night 65
nine 61
no 9
nose 69
not 9
notebook 9
nurse 16

O

o'clock 60
of 28
Oh 15
OK 15
on 12
orange 44

P

paper clip 52
park 72
pen 9
pencil 33
pencil case 8
pet 20
phone 74
piano 64
pin 30
pine 66
pit 30
play 48
playing 70
plays 64
please 42
police officer 16
pony 34
puzzles 10

R

rabbits 11
reach 33
read 56
red 20

refrigerator 27
rice 66
ride 34
robot 54
ruler 9
run 38
running 70

S

sad 15
salad 44
same 48
sandwich 44
school 61
see 6
seven 60
she 16
she's 16
shopkeeper 16
shoulder 69
sick 14
sing 34
sink 27
sit 30
six 60
sleep 56
sleeping 70
snake 48
sofa 27
song 7
soon 14
spaghetti 42
speak 34
spiders 11
stone 74
stop 38
store 72
stove 27
street 24
student 16
studies 64
study 64
sun 38
swim 36
swimming 70

T

table 8
take 64
takes 64
talk 64
talks 64
taxi driver 16
teacher 16
teeth 62
telephone 27
telephone number 24
ten 20
thank you 7
thanks 14
that 8
that's 25
the 7
then 69

there 28
there's 28
these 10
they 10
they're 10
thin 30
this 8
those 10
time 60
tired 15
tissue 52
today 15
toe 69
toilet 27
too 14
top 38
tree 56
trick 34
TV 27
twelve 61
twig 30

U

under 29
up 62
use 34

V

van 12
very 15

W

want 42
wants 44
wash 62
washing 68
watch 50,64
watches 64
watching 72
wet 20
what 8
what's 8
where 24
where's 27
white 66
who 16
who's 16
whose 50
window 8
with 74
write 34
wrong 32

Y

yes 9
yo-yo 74
you 6
your 24